The
Weekender
Effect

The
Weekender
Updated Edition # Effect

*Hyperdevelopment
in Mountain Towns*

Robert William Sandford

RMB
rmbooks.com

For information on purchasing bulk quantities of this book, or to obtain media excerpts or invite the author to speak at an event, please visit rmbooks.com and select the "Contact" tab.

RMB | Rocky Mountain Books Ltd.
rmbooks.com
@rmbooks
facebook.com/rmbooks

Cataloguing data available from Library and Archives Canada
ISBN 9781771606103 (softcover)
ISBN 9781771606110 (electronic)

Printed and bound in Canada

We would like to also take this opportunity to acknowledge the traditional territories upon which we live and work. In Calgary, Alberta, we acknowledge the Niitsitapi (Blackfoot) and the people of the Treaty 7 region in Southern Alberta, which includes the Siksika, the Piikuni, the Kainai, the Tsuut'ina, and the Stoney Nakoda First Nations, including Chiniki, Bearpaw, and Wesley First Nations. The City of Calgary is also home to Métis Nation of Alberta, Region III. In Victoria, British Columbia, we acknowledge the traditional territories of the Lkwungen (Esquimalt and Songhees), Malahat, Pacheedaht, Scia'new, T'Sou-ke, and W̱SÁNEĆ (Pauquachin, Tsartlip, Tsawout, Tseycum) peoples.

We acknowledge the financial support of the Government of Canada through the Canada Book Fund and the Canada Council for the Arts, and of the province of British Columbia through the British Columbia Arts Council and the Book Publishing Tax Credit.

Disclaimer
The views expressed in this book are those of the author and do not necessarily reflect those of the publishing company, its staff, or its affiliates.

----

*To people everywhere who have sacrificed
socially and economically for the places
in which they live and to which their
identity is inextricably tied*

Contents

Foreword to the new edition — IX

Preface — XVII

Standing history on its head — 1

Our greatest cultural achievement — 13

Home place and homesickness — 25

When landscape pervades the psyche — 31

Affirming a sense of place — 37

Threats to mountain place — 45

Painful lessons from my hometown — 53

When words fail: the consequences — 79

The "amenity migration" spin — 87

Saving the West we have — 91

Mounting a different kind of protest — 97

Recovering and rebuilding — 103

Becoming native to place — 111

Bookshelf — 114

Foreword to the new edition

In 2008, I wrote a small book called *The Weekender Effect: Hyperdevelopment in Mountain Towns*. The book was published by Rocky Mountains Books as the first volume in their "manifesto series" of short, concise and well-informed books on matters related to environment and culture.

My concern, and the reason I wrote the book, was that the town in which I lived was under invasion from the outside. It was becoming apparent that if locals didn't wake up to what was happening, we would, without our consent or even our knowledge, end up sacrificing long-established local values, places and cherished local sense of place, to faceless outside interests. While some locals, especially in the rapidly swelling local real estate and development sectors, welcomed and encouraged outside investment in an ever-expanding market for weekend retreats and second homes, the people who established the unique community character of the town were starting to realize that, if not somehow moderated, the sheer scale and pace of change could lead to alienation of many who, though not opposed to change, did not welcome what they saw their town becoming. Many were already finding the place so changed from what they wanted their town to be that they no longer had any reason or incentive to stay. The deeper I looked, however, the more troubling my findings. Locals were literally being dispossessed of qualities of place they didn't realize they had and valued until outside speculators quietly and sometimes secretly robbed them of them by commodifying them and promising them, for a price, to too many outside others.

There were two very polar responses to the book. As anticipated, people in the real estate business and their partners in the development sector hated the book. What surprised me was not that there was also a great deal of local support for the book – I knew that I had found words to describe a growing anxiety long-time locals, especially, felt about the post-Olympics future of the town – but that readers in many other mountain and resort towns, not just in Canada and the United States but in places in Europe and Australia, wrote to say they were under siege by precisely the same outside speculative forces. It soon became clear that a trend was emerging globally. The last best places are being carefully targeted by the world's wealthy elite, and their agents, as super-prime destinations where they can park and grow their wealth. Owned vacancy is now so widespread and the resulting market volatility it creates so disruptive and erosive that it is destabilizing many of the communities they have targeted.

I realize now that there were some things I got wrong in *The Weekender Effect*. The first big thing I got wrong is that I completely underestimated the contribution that many weekenders and retirees would make to the positive development and evolution of the town. Many of these people brought exceptional skills and a broad range of often very specialized experience and competence with them, which they have generously offered to the community.

What I also missed was the potential emergence of whole neighbourhoods of these people who are now reaffirming community values on their own unique terms on the streets in which they live. What I did not anticipate was just how deeply persistent sense of place would remain in many of the people who have resisted being overwhelmed by change in this town and this valley. Another thing I got wrong is that I underestimated the power of this landscape to continue to inspire a new generation of local artists, musicians, writers and filmmakers.

But there are some things in *The Weekender Effect* that, judging from what has happened in the 14 years since I wrote it, I did not get wrong. Too many people have come here too quickly for the community to naturally absorb. Many of the people who live here have little reason to live here, at least in terms of deep and meaningful connection to the place itself. The pandemic and the ease with which many can now work remotely have added to these pressures. Many among this influx may have some feeling for the mountains as backdrop, but they have little connection to the vast region in which they live, and only a fledgling sense of mountain place. For many, the prestige of having a second or third home in a tiny mountain town is the only reason for being here. For a good many others, it is merely a good, solid speculative investment. That there are so many here who are only here to commodify and then mine the landscape and the value of place is exactly what we didn't want. This continues to have unforeseen consequences.

Since I wrote *The Weekender Effect*, the gap between those who have a great deal and those who have far, far less has grown exponentially. In addition, there is a lot less place to have a sense of, and fewer and fewer locals have the abundant time they once had to pursue a deep, personal sense in a mountain landscape that weekenders and outside others appear to be turning into a gymnasium for mechanized sports.

It can no longer be denied that by commodifying place and dramatically increasing the wealth disparity among its citizenry, we are indeed diminishing where we live.

By pushing the ecological limits of where we live, developing every possible empty space and eliminating affordable housing that could be occupied by locals who genuinely want to live here for authentic reasons related to their own identity but cannot afford even one house here, we are robbing ourselves of true community. And we are not done yet. At full build-out to the extent outside developers have proposed, there will be precious little Montane habitat left and less and less room for wildlife, or for people.

Given these circumstances, there are not only bound to be – there should be and already are – tensions. And yet we remain largely oblivious here to how lucky we are. Most of the rest of the world would give anything to have what we are giving up – what we are, in effect, squandering.

Is there hope? Of course. But hope is not something someone gives to us. It is something we have to earn. In the more than a decade since I wrote this book, my argument has not changed. We should not be satisfied to simply accept what we get or what outside others would thrust upon us.

What was worthwhile to the founding generations of locals in the mountain West may not exist much longer unless we take care in teaching newcomers and subsequent generations the historical lessons that took us centuries to learn. Principal among those lessons is that in this landscape our identity can never be completely defined by development. Our true wealth does not reside in what we have built, but in what we have saved; and what we have saved may now save us.

Is it too late? No, at least not here, not yet. But, as I say in the sequel to this book, we need to hurry. The last best West remains under siege. We are witnessing a great bonfire of heritage we didn't know we had. Things are being lost that have not yet been found. We need to find them before they, and we, are lost.

Preface

Deep and meaningful connections to place are a fundamental element of what makes us human. Contemporary economic and geographical mobility are altering our relationship to where we live and changing human settlement patterns, particularly in the mountain West. While academics categorize this large and troubling movement of wealth toward upland regions as "amenity migration," the term inadequately characterizes the devastating impact such movement is having on the integrity of many mountain places. Mountain and other communities, under siege from self-interested outside economic influences that would dispossess locals, need to examine very carefully their roots in history and place and the value of local habits and traditions before they relinquish control of their landscapes and culture to outsiders who would put their communities' heritage up for auction to other outsiders. Only by clearly articulating and defending local values can a community argue successfully against the tyranny of established economic logic and language to preserve the opportunity that still exists to create the West we want.

I have spent the better part of a lifetime articulating and sharing the nature, history and culture of the Canadian Rockies. During that time, I helped organize a number of large-scale heritage celebrations that involved the participation of communities throughout the mountain West. These included centennial commemorations of mountaineering and other historical events, celebrations related to expanding understanding of such wildlife icons as grizzly bears, and initiatives aimed at improving understanding of mountains as headwaters.

Quite by accident, this work put into relief commonalities between what locals thought were very different, sometimes even rival, communities. For a time I felt I had my finger on the pulse of place, at least in the Western mountains in Canada. I found that, beneath all of the rhetoric and spin offered by developers and tourism boosters, the people who lived in these mountains shared a surprisingly deep love of fundamental elements of place. I also discovered that this deep, passionate and powerful sense of localness has only barely been articulated and only superficially harnessed in support of community development and pride. This sense of localness is not always or primarily aligned. It is not pro-business or pro-environment per se. It is before all of that. If anything it is pro-place and pro-community.

Despite this discovery, I cannot claim that my work has been very successful. I sometimes feel as though I have witnessed in a single lifetime the destruction of many of the elements of place and community that gave meaning and value to living in the mountain communities upon which I have, one way or another, depended for my livelihood. But the news I have received from places I have come to know well is not all bad. While observing loss, I have been witness also to glimmerings of great possibility emerging in new visions of the West we want.

Standing history on its head

As a lifelong student of natural and human history, I do not think it unreasonable to make bold new claims about the history of Canada's mountain West. I believe we have a false sense of history, not just in the Rockies but also in the Purcells, Selkirks, Monashees and Cascades. I believe we have derived the wrong lessons from the past and that it is time to stand Western Canadian history on its head.

My first new claim is that we have got our history backward. Our greatest cultural achievement in the mountain region of Western Canada is not what we think it is. It is not what we have developed in terms of infrastructure, industry, commerce or human population growth that has in the end defined us. While we always marked development as central to our history as we have traditionally defined it, railways, highways, towns and cities only partly define our contemporary identity.

My second claim is that the products of the human desire to modify and urbanize the places we live in – whose shape we are so proud of – will not define our identity in the future in the same ways that they will in so many other places in Canada. The mountain West is different from the rest of the country – and from most of the rest of the continent – in that it is not what we constructed out of the landscape that most deeply and enduringly defines us as a people. It is not what we built that truly makes us unique as a culture, but what we saved.

Ask any of the tens of thousands of outsiders that are flocking here to live and they will tell you the same thing. It is not what we built here that is attracting them, but what we protected, not just in terms of landscape but also in terms of culture. What we built only serves to make what we saved meaningful. What we saved in terms of landscape and the right to experience and enjoy it in some semblance of its original character is what makes the West habitable. It is also what makes it attractive to others.

We have saved something in this part of the country that has been lost elsewhere in Canada and widely around the world. In the midst of fragmenting and developing the mountain West, we recognized there were qualities of place here that meant something more to us than immediate wealth. Slowly and haltingly we undertook steps that would allow elements of the West we cherished to be preserved and protected. After discovering what we had, we began to put what we'd already started to destroy back together again in a semblance of its original pristine form.

Another, less bold, assertion I would like to make is that in protecting the spine of the Rocky Mountains we have preserved ecological functions that will be of inestimable value in the future. Not only have we slowed the ecosystem diminishment and species loss that have so affected our continent since the end of the last ice age, we have also kept alive an ecological thermostat that may well be an important defence against future human use and climate change impacts in the Canadian West.

While our efforts to restore what we had damaged, once we saw its great value, are less well known than the history of development, they may in the end be far more important to our identity and our future. Something clearly different happened in the mountain West. Instead of simply overwhelming place and developing it into something it wasn't before, locals accommodated the landscape and allowed it in part to define local character and culture. What makes the foundation of culture in the mountain West unique is the extent to which locals have historically cared about the landscapes in which they live and the degree of ritual and actual sacrifice they are prepared to make to ensure that qualities of place endure from one generation to the next. It is this very process, however, that currently is under threat.

To appreciate the role that what we saved may play in defining this culture we have to understand the efforts that have been made in the past to create this foundation. It is my contention that these efforts began quietly with a local appreciation of landscape experience that led over time to the creation of the individual mountain national and provincial parks that today are clustered along the Great Divide in the Canadian Rockies. Each of these acts of creation was undertaken because locals wanted something more than a West overwhelmed by established forms of development. No one attempted to anticipate – or could even have imagined at the time – how remarkably important the creation of each element in this network of parks would ultimately become.

The first of these small reserves, of course, was Banff. Created in 1885, it was our nation's first national park. It was followed in 1886 by Yoho and in 1907 by Jasper National Park. Mount Robson Provincial Park was created in 1913 and Mount Assiniboine in 1922. Kootenay National Park came into existence in 1923 and was followed by Hamber Provincial Park in 1941. Then the Second World War and its aftermath froze the creation of protected places until prosperity and the increased mobility brought about by the widespread availability of automobiles made it possible for more Canadians and their guests to see and enjoy the spectacular natural wealth that had been preserved.

Once the pieces were saved, it gradually occurred to us that their collective value was far greater than the sum of their parts. It took nearly a century for the value of what we had done to soak in. The Western mountain landscape simply kept dazzling us season after season, generation after generation.

In time, though, the amazing uniqueness of what we had always possessed was put into relief by what others had done to the rest of the West and the rest of the world. Gradually, it became very apparent that we had somehow saved what the rest of the West and the rest of the planet had forgone. We, here, still had a place, and a culture defined by place.

The idea of recognizing the global significance of the remarkable features encompassed within this national and provincial parks network first found expression in 1982. In that year the Burgess Shale in Yoho National Park in British Columbia was identified as one of this country's first UNESCO World Heritage Sites. It was with good reason this site was recognized.

The most productive outcrops of Burgess Shale can be found some 200 metres above the highline trail that overlooks Emerald Lake in Yoho National Park. The first to understand the significance of these fossils was Dr. Charles Doolittle Walcott, the secretary of the

Smithsonian Institution, who literally stumbled upon them during a visit to the Rockies in 1909. Walcott, arguably the foremost American geologist of his time, recognized instantly the importance of his find. Between 1909 and 1911, Walcott collected and exported to Washington, DC, some 65,000 specimens from a quarry on the shoulder of Mount Field, representing some 170 species of plants and animals.

Over the next century, four generations of paleontologists studied the nearly perfectly preserved creatures of the Burgess Shale. One of the greatest of these was a scientist from the Royal Ontario Museum named Desmond Collins. Collins and his colleagues and students mined the Burgess quarry for nearly twenty years. It was based on his testimony about the value of this 543-million-year-old treasure trove to our understanding of Cambrian life that the Burgess Shale was nominated as a World Heritage Site.

For the first twenty years after the site was designated in 1982, everyone seemed satisfied that the rare creatures discovered there had been fully appreciated for what they told us about the evolution of life on Earth. Then, in 2003, a British paleontologist named Andrew Parker caused the Cambrian to explode all over again.

Using an electron microscope to examine the finest features of particularly well-preserved Burgess fauna, Parker discovered the remnants of diffraction gradients in the fossil remains of three Burgess creatures: *Wiwaxia*, *Canadia* and *Marrella*. The presence of diffraction gradients suggested that these animals were iridescent in colour. But what did this mean, Parker asked himself, especially in terms of the Big Bang of evolution that was the Cambrian explosion?

Well, he reasoned, if there was colour, then there must have been light. And if there was light and colour, then these animals could "see." The capacity to see meant the existence of an eye. What Andrew Parker had discovered was that the Big Bang of evolution that took place between 544 million and 543 million years ago was the result of nothing less than the sudden appearance of sight in nature. The Burgess Shale is of inestimable value to us today because it is one of only a tiny number of places on our planet where fossils tell the tale of how nature turned the light switch on.

With the rise of the eye, evolution got out of first gear. At the Cambrian boundary, predators suddenly could come looking for you, and of course this new sense demanded adaptive strategies for prey seeking escape. New musculature appeared. So did jaws and teeth, prickles and shells. And besides all the armament, there also arose ornament: adaptive coloration made its appearance.

In a world where animals could suddenly see, there was an explosion of new niches that life could fill. A broader food web came into existence, which led to the rise of the first true ecosystems, which led to early animals with backbones – chordates like *pikaia* – which led to the vertebrates, which led to us.

Close your eyes. Keep them closed. Now open them again. The world became ours the moment the first eye opened. The emergence of sight caused an advancement of evolution more rapid than had ever occurred before. In only a million years, the world had changed forever. Though vision arose in only six of the 38 phyla that exist today, 95 per cent of all modern animals possess it. This is why the Burgess Shale is so important. And the site is only one of countless wonders of international significance that exist in the Canadian Rockies.

In 1984 the four mountain national parks – Banff, Jasper, Kootenay and Yoho – were, based on the remarkable geological features they protected, granted designation together as a UNESCO World Heritage Site. But that was only a prelude to a grander designation that was to follow six years later. In 1990 the three surrounding British Columbia provincial parks – Mt. Assiniboine, Hamber and Mt. Robson – were added to the mountain national parks under an expanded designation that created one of the most remarkable and significant large-scale ecological and cultural reserves in the world. But once again it took time to fully recognize what we have. It has taken nearly 20 years to realize that the creation of the Canadian Rocky Mountain Parks World Heritage Site is one of the greatest collective expressions of the will to protect national heritage the world has ever witnessed. Though we haven't celebrated it yet, this designation also represents one of the clearest expressions of the desire to preserve the places upon which local cultures depend for their inspiration and authenticity that has ever been articulated in the history of this continent.

Our greatest cultural achievement

What Canada has done in association with
UNESCO and the International Union for the
Conservation of Nature is cause for a cautious
optimism that is increasingly rare in our time.
Though we may not actually have intended
to, we have managed somehow, in just over a
century, to take torn fragments of the larger
Canadian Rockies ecosystem and put them
back together again to recreate a grand tapestry
of our natural and cultural heritage. We have
affirmed our commitment both to our culture
and to the landscapes that make our culture in
the mountain West unique. From this act and
its downstream consequences we can learn much
that we can share with the rest of the world.

No other country in the world has been able to achieve what we have done by way of this remarkable restoration. We have made ourselves whole as a culture by restoring the places that have in the past meant the most to our identity. We have done so by allowing jurisdiction to serve us rather than divide us. And yet, even today, not all of us fully realize just what this accomplishment means. Between 1885 and 1941, we caused what was at first a patchwork of tiny and isolated protected places to coalesce into a contiguous system that now encompasses 2,440,568 hectares – more than 24,405 square kilometres – of some of the most spectacular mountain landscapes in North America. Only now are we beginning to understand the importance of what we have preserved, to imagine what this bold act might mean to our future.

Beyond its sheer scale, perhaps the thing that is most amazing about the Canadian Rocky Mountain Parks World Heritage Site and its surrounding buffers is that it essentially encompasses only one biogeographical and cultural region. Those who live in it recognize it as a region that is spectacular beyond belief. The site encompasses four National Parks, three Provincial Parks, 13 National Historic Sites, four Canadian Heritage Rivers and 27 distinct mountain ranges. Within it are at least 669 prominent peaks and hundreds of outliers and lesser peaks that remain unnamed.

The protection of this mountain region leads to another bold new historical claim, this one relating to the fundamental importance of water to the Canadian West and the role that the Canadian Rocky Mountain Parks World Heritage Site plays as the principal watershed of much of the continent. These mountains function as the water towers of the entire West. Within the World Heritage Site's boundaries are 12 major icefields and some 384 glaciers. Within it are also some 295 lakes. But it is the moving waters that matter most. Within this combined reserve are a total 44 rivers and 164 named tributaries. Only two of these rivers are dammed. If this weren't already astounding enough, four of the greatest rivers of North America are born here, and they are what make the downslope West habitable – for us and for the rest of the natural world.

Apart from purely environmental considerations, there is also an economic aspect to this additional claim I would like to make. Although the tourism potential of this expanded protected area is an important element of the Western Canadian economy, the role of this place as healthy watershed will be more important and more valuable to the future than we can even begin to imagine today. More than natural and cultural heritage is preserved within and around this site. Within the broader context of upland watershed protection, the protection of this broad area may also prove to be one of the best land-use decisions we have ever made in Canadian history. With each passing day we learn more about the value of the ecological services nature provides to us for free that would be beyond our means to provide for ourselves. It is now estimated that healthy ecosystems provide clean water and other natural benefits for less than 1 per cent of what those benefits would cost us to generate on our own.

There are other economic reasons as well for considering the value of this expanded protected area. We are quickly learning that ecology is economy. We may soon discover that our decision to preserve our upland watershed in the Rocky Mountains may ultimately allow nature to offer us the best deal it has offered humanity since agriculture: the gift of true sustainability.

Even the gaps that separate watersheds are important. This World Heritage Site encompasses 23 named mountain passes and at least 25 major airsheds. It contains three life zones and is home to more than 600 species of plants, 277 species of birds and 69 species of mammals, including 13 different carnivores. There are some 900 archaeological sites here, some of which evidence the earliest presence of humans, at sites that date from early, middle and late pre-historic times to the present. In historic times the landscape encompassed was within the often overlapping territories of at least 12 First Nations. Parts as well were the home of generations of Métis, people of mixed European and Native blood who formed the foundation of post-contact culture in the Canadian West. The long presence of these peoples contributes inestimably to local culture and sense of place.

Presently there are four permanent communities within this World Heritage Site, with a tightly controlled total resident population of fewer than 20,000. These people live in the World Heritage Site for a reason: to operate and maintain these reserves and to serve and care for visitors. Besides the national parks towns, there are also dozens of towns and a number of major cities that are located so close to the World Heritage Site that their presence interpenetrates the mountain parks and their surrounding buffer zones. The nature and character of Western towns and cities are inseparable from the nature and character of the adjacent mountain landscapes. In the deepest sense of the word, the economies of one define the economies of the other.

So famous is the Canadian Rocky Mountain Parks World Heritage Site that it is the destination of more than seven million visitors every year. But this number is deceptive. Though a million people may crowd Banff Avenue in a year, there also are valleys in and around this World Heritage Site that may be visited once in a decade.

The world is beginning to fully recognize that what we have created in the mountain region of the Canadian West is nothing less than one of the most expansive collective expressions of the will to protect natural heritage the world has ever witnessed. The remarkable nature of this achievement invites Canadians to think in alternative terms about how we might live in association with the remarkable landscape we have allowed nature to bring back into existence in our time. Realization of the dimensions of our accomplishment may also suggest that an opportunity exists now to work consciously toward creating a culture and an economy commensurate with the grand nature of the landscape we have preserved. This great reserve forms a baseline of understanding about the West that puts into relief what existed in the past so that we can appreciate the value of what we possess – and what possesses us – now. In this region, it is still possible to use the past as an immediate foundation for planning for the future.

Recasting our history against the backdrop of such an extraordinary intergenerational public policy achievement gives our culture some room to manoeuvre in a time when natural systems everywhere are under great stress and are changing rapidly. We have not spent all of our natural capital. The fact that we have saved important functioning elements of our natural and cultural history allows us a latitude which others in much of the rest of the world do not possess to choose the future we want. What we have saved keeps the door open to the most important of all cultural options: the opportunity to create a new and inspired vision of what kind of West we would like to create for ourselves and our children. But the West – and the world – is changing quickly. The door to the future we want is not likely to remain open long.

Imagining and then creating the West we want may seem an impossible task. We are faced with significant threats to both our heritage and our future. While we have good reason to be pleased with our long history of achievement in landscape protection in the Canadian Rockies, there are developments now occurring within the World Heritage Site and along its boundaries that have long-time locals concerned at the most fundamental level of relationship to place. What we are doing to our mountain towns should give us pause of long enough duration to at least think about this relationship. Either we establish a vision of the West we want now or our descendants will be forced to live forever with the consequences of a blind incrementalism that will leave them with very little of what made this region such an inspiring place to live in and visit.

Today, in this writer's opinion at least, the processes of change that are reshaping the mountain West are creating a future that is neither intended nor desirable. Certainly, what happened where I live is not what I intended as a Westerner and not at all what I desire. It is my fear that if we do not recognize and respond to the threats to our historic relationship to place, we could lose the West we have and along with it any chance we may still possess to create the West we want. Ironic as it may appear, we run the risk of our great conservation achievements backfiring on us. If we are not careful, the desirable lifestyle and cultural conditions we created by way of what we saved may, in the end, be our undoing.

We cannot let our appreciation of place be rewarded by the emergence of circumstances in which the very people who established the character and quality of life in the mountain West are driven out of the places they love by the urban wealthy. We cannot let our success in creating one of the most desirable places in the world result in our being dispossessed by those who would buy us out and take away from us everything that has meaning in relation to where and how we live.

What we need in order to counter the threats we face at this moment in history is a heightened appreciation for what we already have and a realization of what is possible in the future based on what we have already achieved in the past. History tells us we already know how to employ the power of mountain place in the service of defining a unique Western Canadian identity. We already know that by caring about our mountains we can create the West we want. We have done it once. We can do it again.

Home place and homesickness

The relationship between people and the places they live in is a complicated one. It always has been. In 400 BCE the great Greek physician Hippocrates observed that whenever people from one country were sent distantly to another, they were often beset with a debilitating lassitude.

From this, the father of modern medicine deduced that people absorbed topographic influences from the moment of birth and that separation from those could be perilous. This lassitude he called *nostalgia*. The word has its roots in the Greek *nostos*, to return, and *algos*, to suffer. We call it homesickness.

The first modern sufferers of this "lassitude of dislocation" were 17th-century Swiss mercenaries in the employ of European emperors. Though the Swiss were tough and committed soldiers, they found themselves overcome by lethargy and melancholy the moment they were confronted by the slightest sight, sound or smell that reminded them of Switzerland. It is said that the mere sound of a Swiss cowbell would completely incapacitate them. There are Swiss mountain guides in places like Golden, British Columbia, who are like that even today. The Europeans called this debilitating sense of place "the terrible Swiss disease." This disease became an epidemic over much of the world as people began to migrate to the New World in large numbers in 18th and 19th centuries.

Human population movement has become so rapid and commonplace now that it is easy to forget how stationary people used to be and how connected to place we once were. But the lingering attachment we have to where we were born is not something we can easily dismiss. When Europeans first arrived on the Great Plains and in the mountains of the Canadian West, the experience was so alien and the landscape so overwhelming that for many it was if they were landing on the moon. It took generations for settlers to become at home in this new place. The process required closing a circle of experience, livelihood and story that resulted in the gradual creation of a history, a specific literature of place and finally the creation of art that affirmed connection to place. As Ronald Rees suggested in his landmark book *New and Naked Land: Making the Prairies Home*, this creates an ideal past and a nostalgia for earlier, less complicated times in our lives and in our history.

As Rees suggests, this nostalgia for the past often has as much to do with an unsatisfactory present as it does with how a former way of life has been idealized in memory. More and more this appears to be true in communities in and around the Canadian Rocky Mountain parks.

Attachment to place is not something we seem to be able to shake. When NASA sent astronauts to the moon, they prepared them for the shock of the new by having them study how European immigrants reacted to the alien landscapes of the North American West. Like early pioneers, astronauts have been observed to have re-entry problems associated with the extent to which pressing elements of our unsatisfactory present are put into relief by the image of an ideal world as pictured from space.

Aboriginal peoples were as utterly at home in the landscapes of the mountain West as they were on the Great Plains. Their descendants today must look upon us newcomers as pitifully clumsy in our efforts to come to grips with what is really essential about place in the mountain West. Settlers today must suffer the difficulty of coming to terms with the circumstances and climate of an utterly new place just as their ancestors did. Fitting in and becoming a local takes time, and just as on the plains, there appears to be a process by which newcomers come to terms with their emerging identity in the Rockies. Aboriginal peoples must also find it more than just a little ironic that after taking a century or so to make the West home, the settlers that dispossessed them are now being displaced themselves, this time by wealthy urbanites from around the world who have decided that living in this largely protected landscape is preferable to living in the often crowded and dirty places they helped build.

In a very general way the process of coming to terms with a place is similar to the one Rees describes. Experience of a new and sometimes dangerous landscape and the trials of making a living spawn personal stories. Stories coalesce into legend, which over time becomes the foundation of local history. History spawns literature. Literature begets visual art and art confirms the experience of place. It is a clumsy process with many false starts and wrong turns. Eventually, however, we interlopers gradually applied enough persistence and patience to the project of localness to complete the self-reinforcing cultural circle that allows us to claim the difficult and often dangerous Rockies as home.

This process is central to our unique identity in the mountain West. Once you participate in the larger environment that envelops where you live, you are gradually shaped by it. You come to notice and appreciate it. Gradually the moods and nuances of where you live become yours. The country invades you, so to speak, and you call it home.

Since the expanded Canadian Rocky Mountain Parks World Heritage Site was designated in 1990, we have recognized that we could make our commitment to understanding, appreciating and experiencing where we live the foundation of a sustainable future in the Canadian West. The first step in doing so, however, is to recognize the terms and conditions of our relationship with where we live. The American farmer-philosopher Wendell Berry once claimed that you can't know who you are unless you know where you are. In other words, a sense of belonging to a place matters to our identity as individuals and as communities.

When landscape pervades the psyche

Though it can help a great deal, you can't acquire or keep a sense of place just by reading about it. To be truly open to the uniqueness of country, you have to involve yourself in it physically. Acquiring grace in the mountains is often as much a matter of "letting go" as of conquering the country or conquering your own soul. Though he was not a mountaineer, one of the 20th century's most articulate spokespersons on how we can be transformed by place was T.E. Lawrence.

Better known as Lawrence of Arabia, Thomas Edward Lawrence was an Englishman who possessed what he called "an English love of desolate places." In his book *Seven Pillars of Wisdom*,

Lawrence describes becoming so exhausted, so thirsty and so sun-baked that he could no longer hold his will on his ambitions or his mission. His ego drained out of him. He became will-less and culture-less with exhaustion, hunger and thirst. And at the moment when he could no longer apply his fierce intellect to his task, something amazing happened to him. In a moment of sublime openness, the desert in all its light and wind, in all its timelessness and unity washed over him. He could no longer resist the eternal beauty of the wind and the sun. In an instant the desert changed, and so did he.

Many people have had similar experiences in our mountains. You find yourself too tired to keep the wilderness at bay. You are no longer able to assert your own interests and perspectives. You arrive at a point where all you can hear is your own deep breathing, your heart thumping and the hissing silence of the world. When these sounds subside, you begin to hear again, but you start hearing other things. When the great engine of cultural homogenization we carry around inside us runs out of fuel, there is a profound moment when we can be overwhelmed by landscape, wind and sun. Suddenly we see nature not as something alien but as a unified whole out of which we have emerged.

You can call the acquisition of a sense of place a mindset change. You could call it a paradigm shift or a transcendence of thought and perceptual form. It has also been called epiphany, or aesthetic arrest. Provided that that cultural homogenization dynamo doesn't start up again too soon, the epiphany can last. If it does, a staggering realization sometimes forms inside us: the realization that we are not the centre of everything, that all of nature is holy, too.

It was epiphany of this kind that Aboriginals sought in vision quests. It is this kind of epiphany that today makes ordinary people give up everything they are doing in their lives to move to the mountains and be part of them. It is epiphany of this kind that is at the heart of an inspired sense of place. It is our desire to share such epiphany with others that makes it worth living in and visiting these mountains. It is through the articulation and sharing of our deeper sense of place that we can build sustainable communities in and around the nation state of wonder we created when we married the finest elements of ourselves and our landscapes to create the Canadian Rockies World Heritage Site.

The sharing of a profound appreciation of place is not always easy. If you have had a transformational experience, it can be very difficult to describe it to others. To do so, however, may be one of our most urgent challenges. As the world grows more and more crowded and distracted, there is less opportunity for us to be alone. We have less time to think about who we are and what we would like to be. Under a barrage of global technology and business processes we are all becoming more and more alike, more urban. In such an environment, our sense of place falters. We let the outside world wash over us and we lose our grip on the crumbling rock of where we live.

The global homogenization of culture around urban values is overwhelming the sense of place in the rural mountain West. Habitats that are unique to place, and that allow us to affirm a sense of place, are disappearing at a rate faster than at any other time in history. In the world of comfort and distraction that has replaced the natural world, a sense of place is harder to find and harder to keep. We spend much of our time running to and fro; it is difficult to stay grounded in the details of where we live. Real grounding in place is vanishing from our culture. It is this grounding, however, that we must protect if we are going to make where and how we live the basis of our future.

Affirming a sense of place

The great American writer Wallace Stegner was among the first in North America to call the nostalgia created in our own minds by the landscapes in which we live "a sense of place." Stegner grew up in southern Saskatchewan and returned there after 40 years in the United States to write the definitive book on sense of place on the prairies, *Wolf Willow*. In *Wolf Willow*, and other books such as *The American West as Living Space*, *The Sound of Mountain Water*, *Angle of Repose* and *The Bluebird Sings at Lemonade Springs*, Stegner attempted to define the elements that compose the unique relationship to landscape and culture he called "sense of place." Though American and Canadian writers and critics have attempted to enlarge his categories somewhat, they remain, in effect, as he articulated them. Sense of place, as defined by Stegner, comprises three essential elements.

The first is unique geography. A person can only appreciate a sense of the place where they live if they see the geography of that place as special. As I have said so often, it is hard not to feel that way here. The geography of the Rockies leans in on you; it is hard to ignore. Even unseen in darkness or in storm, the mountains exert a presence. This presence is sometimes subtle, but it can be profound. Often people don't know the physical landscape is reaching into them and making them locals by gradual association if not by choice. But if you stay long enough you see it.

Where I live in the Rockies people often stay only briefly and then move on. I have almost given up establishing close relations with people who come for the summer or for a year, for it breaks my heart to see them constantly leaving just as I got to know and like them. But in departing, they have much to teach about the power of physical landscapes to define a deeper sense of place.

Many people I have known have come to me to explain that they are tired of the tourism-business culture and the high cost of living in resort towns and are leaving, never, as they so often say, to return again. I now make it a habit to reserve judgment, for so many have returned two or three years later to stand sheepishly at my door. Inevitably their story is always the same. They were in some distant mountain range, the Alps, the Andes or perhaps the Himalayas and they became unexpectedly aware of a sight, a sound or a smell that reminded them of home. It might have been the perfume of spring pines, the sulphurous stench of newly broken limestone or the colour and scent of fall leaves. Whatever it was released in them a flood of nostalgia that could only be associated with experiences they had had in the Rockies. At that moment they knew that, like or it not, the

Rockies were their home and that, whatever the sacrifice, they would become locals by choice. The geography had finally captured them and they had come home.

The second element of place, according to Stegner, is a remembered and celebrated history. This history is most often personal or familial. You have to have a history in that place. Perhaps you remember the first time you were overtaken by the smell of pines. Or perhaps you recall the excitement and fear that accompanied your first encounter with a bear. You remember the stream where you caught your first fish. You remember what it felt like to realize that you could be comfortable in the cold and that winter was just another season in which the landscape opened itself to exploration, not just of place but of yourself.

When you remember in this way, you experience the subtle awareness that what actually happens to you in the present is as or more important than the fact that the place around you may have been an exploration route or the site of an early trading post or a particularly interesting section on an early railway line. History starts with us as individuals and then radiates outward toward others. We find our place in local history and then become a mooring for others to do the same. When this happens we often discover that how we live today is not radically different in essence from how those before us lived in this landscape. And where it is different it is at least consistent with experience of place in the past. This realization constitutes yet another step in the process of belonging.

The third step in coming home to place is related to how personal history merges with the larger history of a community and region. It is the application of personal history to contemporary meaning. An informed sense of place requires that what happened in a given place in the past has meaning in the present. In reaching this stage in the adoption of place, you suddenly see yourself as part of a continuum in the life and experience of the community in which you have chosen to live. You are part of that continuum and it is part of you. You see how you live reflected in where you live. Suddenly geology and topography have relevance. Suddenly you see why 10,000 years of Native presence matters. You understand the impact of the coming of the railway, not just on your community but on your life. You see history as a continuum that now not only includes you but affects how you and your neighbours live in your time.

The establishment of this relationship often requires the skilled storytelling of elders or the informed and enthusiastic interpretation of archaeologists and historians, naturalists and artists. And behind all of these we find the guiding hand of community leaders whose role it is to employ public policy to quietly alter the DNA of place to create community adaptability to changing circumstances.

It is in recognition of all these people that I propose to add a fourth element to Wallace Stegner's remarkable list of the components of a refined appreciation of where we live. Every real place features a cast of genuine local characters. These are people steeped in the geography, history and meaning of place who become crystals around which aesthetics are articulated and passed on through time. It is these people who have made sacrifices that have made them truly worthy and utterly representative of where they live. These are people of such unique character that you immediately want to emulate their sincerity and connection to what is truly meaningful about where they live. In these people, sense of place has become a form of grace. The moment you meet them you want to be like them. It is important that such people do not become rare in the mountain West.

Threats to mountain place

While most of us feel an element of grounding in where we live, most will agree that sense of place in our society is not what it used to be. Because of increased mobility, real grounding in place is vanishing from our experience. We have so many distractions, and we spend so much of our time running to and fro, it is sometimes difficult to stay grounded in the sense and fact of place.

Michael Crichton is the well-known author of novels such as *The Andromeda Strain*, *Timeline* and of course *Jurassic Park*. *Jurassic Park* was made into one of my favourite films of all time. In it I find profound symbolism. Imagine, a dinosaur eating a lawyer!

Like many of us, Crichton is an inveterate voyager. In his classic book called *Travels*, he touches on what is happening to our sense of connection with the places we visit:

> … during a trek in Nepal, my Sherpa guide took me to the top of a hill at a place called Ghoripani, pointed to the view and said:
>
> "The Kali-Gandaki Gorge." "Uh-huh," I said. I was sweating and tired. It was cold. My feet hurt. I could hardly pay attention to this view.
>
> "The Kali-Gandaki Gorge," he repeated significantly. "Uh-huh," I said. What I was seeing wasn't even a gorge, it was just a big valley with snowy mountain peaks on both sides. Spectacular, but all the mountain views in Nepal are spectacular, and I was tired at the end of the day.
>
> "The Kali-Gandaki Gorge," he said a third time. Like I still wasn't getting the point. "Great," I said. "When's dinner?"

It wasn't until I returned home that I found out what the Kali-Gandaki Gorge is.

The Kali-Gandaki River cuts between the peaks of Dhaulagiri to the west and Annapurna to the east, respectively the sixth- and tenth-highest mountains in the world.

Both peaks rise more than four miles above the river below, making a canyon so enormous that the eye can hardly see it for what it is. It is four times as deep as the Grand Canyon, and far wider; between the peaks you could roughly fit twenty Grand Canyons.

The Kali-Gandaki Gorge is the deepest canyon in the world. That's what it is. I'd like to go back and see it some time.

As mentioned before, you can't acquire a sense of place just by reading about it. To be truly open to the uniqueness of country, you have to involve yourself physically in it. Sense of place is only established when a relationship to a specific landscape or culture captures you and makes you a local by choice. I know this because it happened to me.

Despite these discoveries, I cannot claim I have been very successful in making sense of place an element we consider in determining what kind of future we want in the mountain West.

As historian Donald Worster has pointed out, human adaptation to nature is never simply a matter of technological application and practical inventiveness. If that were so, then the most highly technological societies that presently exist in the world would have the least impact on their physical environments. In fact, the contrary is true: it is precisely our most technological societies that appear to possess the least respect for natural limits and that practise the least environmental restraint.

Increasingly in our time, however, we are seeing that technology and development cannot improve a place in the absence of a deeply felt local sense of the natural order.

The most enduring communities are those in which the identity of the self and the character of the community became indistinguishable from the nature of the land and the fabric of life that supports the uniqueness of place. This can only emerge locally from a sense of place that is at once an understanding of what makes a landscape function as it does and a feeling of belonging to and sharing in its uniqueness. As Worster put it, sense of place is a special adaptiveness that emerges when the individual reflects the community and the community reflects the landscape in which it is embedded, and out of these interdependencies there emerges a unique and local cultural ecology.

Over the past century our mountain communities have been absorbed slowly into the landscape, creating just the kind of relationship to place that might allow us to endure here, but now that is changing. Many mountain communities no longer pace themselves to a self-generated, self-contained rhythm of local place. Instead, we pace ourselves to the rhythms of disruptive urban excitements and economic interests that have little to do with local character and sense of place.

Living in the mountains, we are still close enough to the roots of our past that we may still hear the siren call of the great lone land. But as urban lifestyles continuously accelerate, people increasingly desire the monumental in nature without having to spend hours or days to find it in the landscape or in themselves. Even a landscape compromised by logging or mining is a relative wilderness for someone who comes from Toronto, Tokyo or New York. People are flocking to natural and semi-natural tourism destinations and resort communities because the urban places they live in are becoming less and less desirable. In many cases, the urban invasion is making the places they flock to uninhabitable too. Pleasant tourism terms like "amenity migration" do not accurately portray what's happening, particularly in the mountain

West. The wealthy everywhere in the world are, in fact, becoming a first wave of environmental refugees seeking the highest quality of life in non-urban environments. Many of the last best places are under siege.

When the original character of place is gone, and the presence of more and more people makes it harder to enjoy that character for those who come later, the kind of people who come changes. Marketing no longer stresses place, but instead focuses on material culture as expressed by status symbol. Shoppers replace hikers and these shoppers justify more shops. Now that a local grounding in place is gone, the tourists hurry on. They have no reason to visit places that are as compromised as what they already have at home. They just pass through on their way to the next "last best place." It is the weekenders who stay.

As anyone who has travelled for any length of time in the Canadian Rockies will know, the qualities of place Westerners have established here over time have become very attractive to outsiders. Over the last ten years, almost every community along the spine of the Rockies, from Aspen to Valemount, has experienced the same growing influx. People come from the US, from the Pacific coast, from Ontario or from cities in Alberta and they fall in love with the mountain way of life – and they want to stay. At least for the weekend. Some communities have adjusted to this. Others have not. I come from one that hasn't.

Painful lessons from my hometown

I live in a mountain town that has an interest-ing and representative history. Like many rural communities in the Western mountains, this town was founded on a resource-based economy. Though idealists tend to give mining towns a miss, being a resource-based community is not necessarily or always a bad thing in the context of evolving sense of place. Before I arrived, four generations of coal miners had created a very solid community. A focus on family values and common experience related to the mine had become the foundation of shared identity. The neighbourliness they created and enjoyed can only be found in small towns. There was an unconditional willingness to help one another in times of crisis and to celebrate with one another in times of joy.

Unfortunately, people in communities like these, especially if they are located in spectacular places, are often forced by economic realities to give way to outsiders who capitalize on a vision that locals were unable to see or completely articulate or perhaps just couldn't afford. When the coal mines closed, many people believed it was the end of the town. Locals were frightened. Politicians at the time argued the town should actively pursue any development that would provide it with a tax base and a foundation for some sort of future. Anything would do as long as it translated into economic development. We forgot that trees grow back and the wounds mining make on the landscape scar over in time and even heal. We didn't pay attention to what had happened to mining towns in attractive mountain places elsewhere along the Great Divide.

The vast majority of people who lived in this town were locals by choice. Three generations of locals had sacrificed to be made whole and unique by the place in which they lived. In other words, this town was a real place. We believed, at that time, that the traditions of community created during a century of mining made the place where we lived remarkable in its own right. We thought we should at all costs preserve the small-town values that made it rewarding to live in our valley.

We also believed that, with time and a little business training, locals could gradually establish a new economy around the sharing of spectacular nearby landscapes and local culture with visitors. To some extent, this happened, but something else happened, too. Growth got away from us. In less than half a generation, we built a new town five times the size of the one I moved to 27 years before. In 1981, when I arrived, the population was 3,100. By 1990, the population had increased by 71 per cent to 5,300. In 2000, just ten years later, our town had grown a further 98 per cent to 10,500. At the time of this writing, nearly a decade into the new millennium, the population is about

15,000 and still growing. That is a 480 per cent increase in population since I moved here.

Though statistics give an indication of the extent of change, they barely begin to explain the impact of such rapid growth on community identity and dynamics. The rate of growth over the last decade has outstripped the community's ability to reorganize itself around change. Development of local community values and sense of place has not kept pace with construction and physical development. The community has begun to wobble under the weight of its own substantial but unequal development. Visitors or former locals who return after long absences invariably observe that the town has altered itself almost beyond recognition. The rate and extent of change has left many long-term residents in a state of shock.

The town has become essentially urban in character. We now have traffic jams, weekend gridlock and parking problems. There are multilight waits at downtown intersections, long lines of cars and trucks at railway crossings and, perhaps not surprisingly, the appearance of a completely new phenomenon: road rage. Everything is being turned into a money-making proposition. Every square centimetre of property is for sale. Condominiums are sprouting out of every open space. Much-hated photo radar traps are operated not by the police but by commercial privateers who hide in places that ensure big profits but do little for traffic safety. The town is now pondering additional insults such as parking meters. Weekenders don't even notice – they are used to it – but locals still hanging on to their ideal of community don't like it one bit.

The biggest problems, however, are not tied to traffic or privatized policing. They relate to the local cost of living. Many of the people who established the nature and desirable character of this community can no longer afford to live here. Other long-time residents argue the town has changed so much that they no longer feel they belong. At the time of this writing fully half of the population has lived here less than five years. This tells us that as the population continues to grow, locals are on the way out.

The high cost of living also affects other community dynamics. Many newer residents are too busy making a living to have time to become involved civically and be accepted in the community. While they have homes here, they are too busy making ends meet to actually "live" while they are here. There are also many others who enjoy enough wealth that they can have homes in our community without needing to actually live here.

There are subdivisions here now that have so few people living in them full time that they lack the basic elements that by definition constitute functional community life. Big houses exist side by side but there is not enough interaction between those who occupy them to constitute community as we have known it historically in the mountain West. Imagine what would be upscale neighbourhoods anywhere else in the world occupied by residents a few days or weeks each year and one gets the sense of how vacuous such places can be. In the midst of all of this are those whose families founded the town and defined the qualities of community and place that made it so attractive to the weekenders and time-sharers that have now overwhelmed it. Outnumbered remaining locals, who survived the transition from a coal mining community to what the town is today, have few illusions about the future. They know their children will never be able to live in the town they themselves grew up in unless their children have parental or family help or they hit it rich somewhere else and come back. Many parents are barely hanging on, themselves, and the writing is already on the wall for their children.

Whether we care to admit or not, this has created a growing tension between wealthy retirees who own second and third homes and struggling locals who justifiably feel they are being pushed out of their own town. This tension is only heightened by outsiders insensitive to the damage they are causing to what were established local community values. Many newcomers have been wealthy or comfortably retired for so long that they can't imagine people with real lives having trouble making ends meet in the town they have claimed by their numbers and their desires as their own.

In avoiding conflict, respect is important. New residents and especially weekenders may not always appreciate that local traditions may have evolved in diametric opposition to the values, attitudes and habits they are bringing in, without much thought, from away. Newcomers forget that people who moved here before the boom cherish the town not because it offers good investment opportunities, but because it is the one place in the world that permitted them to be who they wanted to be.

Because of their success back where they really live, many newcomers also act as if they have easy solutions to local problems. Inadvertently and unavoidably, many of the solutions they impose will be perceived as turning our community into the kind of place these new people just left. With money, energy and growing numbers on their side, new residents and active weekenders gain the upper hand. Soon, long-time locals are reduced to playing the final, irrefutable and rather ridiculous card that is length of residence. "I know because I have been here longer than you." While this gambit can permit long-time locals a brief wallow in self-righteousness, its ultimate effect can be demonstrably counterproductive. Claiming cultural superiority based on length of residence can make newcomers feel bad about how they have disrupted local community values and sense of place. Unfortunately, it is usually only those people who are already sensitive to place and have come for all the right reasons who notice such concerns. The new people you would want to become a vital part of your community – the ones who are willing to make the ritual and actual sacrifices to place to be worthy of absolute acceptance – are often the ones who are hurt most by the longevity claims of long-standing locals. As a result they can hold back their neighbourliness, their appreciation of place and their commitment to its future to the detriment of what the community might become in its next and seemingly inevitable iteration.

The outsiders you wish had not come, however, are often the ones that are the most oblivious to such claims. They are not around enough to hear them and may not be connected enough even to the places where they do live to understand what a case for localness in what they consider a weekend or resort town might mean, even if those making that case were able to articulate it well enough to make sense to one another and to others.

Recently a long-time local told a very poignant story about her experience of the changing character of her community. This woman had been invited to a lavish party thrown by a wealthy weekender in honour of one of his local friends.

Her very generous host was lamenting that he and his wife had chosen to move to this valley because of the excellent relationships they had developed in the local outdoor adventure community. Now that he and his family had moved here to be a bigger part of that community, he was saddened to discover that many of the people he had moved here to be near were leaving. Standing beside this successful, affable and well-meaning man, the woman simply didn't have the heart to tell him that he was part of the reason why the people who had made our community desirable for him could no longer afford to live here. It would have crushed him.

Without a specific focus or vision of what a community might become at its desired future best, it can take years for the character of a town to catch up with the fact of its own rapid and expansive development. It can take years for newcomers who do care very much about the place they have chosen to live in, to feel they belong. It may take a lifetime or two to overcome the hurt caused unnecessarily by too much growth in too short a time. It may take a new generation of locals who do not live with the pain of the past but in the realities of the present to create a desirable future.

Or else the potential for a positive future that respects the past may simply be lost.

So what did we do wrong in the town I live in and what can other communities in and around the Western mountain parks learn from it?

The first thing other communities in similar potential circumstances should learn is that it is important to take these kinds of threats seriously.

Despite the fact that we had expert advice and were personally knowledgeable about what had happened to so many mountain communities in the American Rockies, we simply couldn't grasp the fact that what had happened elsewhere could happen here. We simply refused to believe that people from elsewhere who did not care to the same depth about our mountains and the way of life that had emerged around deep respect for them could suddenly seize control of where we lived and turn it into something diametrically opposite to what we thought appropriate and meaningful. It didn't occur to us until it was too late that the enemy wasn't growth so much as the deeply ingrained habit everywhere in the West of continually delaying action on ecological decline and loss of local grounding in sense of place until further growth has satisfied what are perceived to be more urgent agendas.

The second thing we did wrong was that we didn't recognize the extent to which real estate speculation would mask itself as tourism development. We did exactly what writer Rick Bass argued we shouldn't do. We let the most meaningful elements of place "be divided up into halves, and then quarters and then eighths"; then we further divided what was left into "the invisibility of neglect and loss."

The third thing we did wrong was that we did not have enough faith in ourselves, our values or the grandeur of the landscape around us. Because we were so afraid of missing out on all-important economic development – of any kind – it didn't occur to us that what we already had was of great value. We didn't realize until too late that we had choices. We failed to realize that we had already created the foundation for the development of the most extraordinary mountain community in North America and that the outsiders who wanted to trade on our values were only trying to make as much money as they could and then sell out and leave. Because we failed to appreciate what we already had, we let our town be swallowed up by outsider self-interest. I wish I could say they just walked in and took our town away from us, but that is not entirely true. There were insiders involved and they profited, sometimes very handsomely, from helping us give it away.

The fourth thing we did wrong was that concerned citizens were far too nice. Being pleasant, honest and trusting people, we did not believe outside interests would exploit our generosity and sincerity through expensive, expertly orchestrated and quietly manipulative public relations manoeuvres that we later discovered had been widely employed elsewhere in the Rockies where similar speculation in real estate had already eroded locals' values and sense of place.

The main vehicle for activating our vulnerability to outside public relations strategies was the collaborative process. Large-scale growth management and community visioning exercises confirmed to locals that Brooklyn Dodgers manager Leo Durocher was essentially right when in 1946 he declared that nice guys finish last. Up until we had to fight for our local values, however, we thought we had created the kind of community where no one had to finish last.

A feature of these processes was that everyone involved was expected to suspend their mistrust of the way special interests had begun to hijack public policy in our community in the hope that reasoned dialogue would somehow lead to positive change over the long term. The suspension of mistrust takes specific forms, the most universal of which is the acceptance that participants are all bound by the promise of collaboration to ignore or temporarily deny some of the things they see happening right in front of their very eyes in order to achieve future benefit and harmony.

I have never been involved in a collaborative process anywhere, however, in which private, moneyed interests did not prolong the proceedings in order to use that time to manipulate public process, in some cases almost surgically, to their own ends. In our contemporary corporate milieu, ecological values and conservation practices are only accepted where and insofar as they help business achieve its growth goals. Public relations tricks are employed in ways designed to exhaust any opposition through a war of attrition on local values. Collaborative processes employed in the planning and development of the town I live in paralyzed any hope of a tenable future for locals by killing any practical vision of the future that was not consistent with the extent and character of the growth proposed by the largely outside development community. "Growth management" strategies were turned into their exact opposite by the very length of time it took to articulate and then implement threshold monitoring standards. By the time such baselines for measuring the impacts of growth were finally in place, the horses of growth had already been loosed from the regulatory corral in the quiet of the political night. They can now be found feeding everywhere.

There was also outside interference. The government of the province I live in manipulated the very laws constraining local control over such growth in order to ensure that the greatest good to the greatest number of developers trumped local community values and connection to place. But the fact that area structure plans and other planning vehicles had already left the station before the average local could get up and shovel their sidewalk was not deemed enough to mollify local faith in political process and destroy our belief in the possibility of a different vision of the future. Outside interests were not interested in partial victory. Near annihilation was required.

To reform the community into a different image of itself, long-standing local community solidarity had to be shattered. Outside forces could play a role reforming local values, but total restructuring could only be accomplished from within. As the development community suggested time and again, if you want an omelette, you have to be prepared to break a few eggs. Where I live, however, not everyone bought into this bromide. In long-established mountain communities where local identity is often founded on hard-won individuality, not everyone is eager to sacrifice what is unique and meaningful about their life simply to satisfy the homogenizing financial interests of outside speculators. Many locals were incensed that they were being likened to eggs and their community turned into a timeshare omelette. A significant portion of the community, it was discovered, possessed no appetite for what the developers wanted to make of their community and could not be made to trill excitedly at the prospect of being served up as a cooked carrot on a lavish portfolio menu eyed briefly at an investors brunch in some foreign city.

The developers, however, knew just what to do to solve this problem. They would let conspicuous wealth do what needed to be done to ensure their interests would remain unfettered. The fact that some locals, particularly landowners and an emerging real estate agent class, were making a lot of money at the expense of where and how people had lived in our community for generations gradually divided the community against itself. It should never be forgotten that envy and greed remain powerful and highly divisive community forces. Soon many locals who were already suspicious of developers were also suspicious of the mayor, the town, newcomers and ultimately of one another. For many it was but a short step to being suspicious of everyone.

We later discovered that this "divide and conquer" strategy was just one more standard public relations ploy to which our community had been subjected. Its common use elsewhere proved galling to many of us who felt we should have been smart enough to see when we were being manipulated. I am stunned, in retrospect, by how easy it was to create mutual mistrust within our own community and how naturally even I fell into the trap of questioning the motives of others in whom I had once invested deep trust when our shared community values came under threat from well-financed and well-organized external interests. As the unspoken bond that had previously united us in pursuit of qualities of community that made where and how we live inseparable came under increasing assault, we began to genuinely distrust one another, and we continue to do so to this day.

In the meantime, the sloppily built timeshare ghettos continued to be blessed by the urbanites that now populated our town's unimaginative and uninspired planning department and were developed so quickly, at such high densities and with so little thought, that they often closed off one another's promised views of the surrounding peaks.

Looking back more than a decade later we realize just how effectively some of the simplest public relations tricks that were employed on us worked. One of the best ones was actually a joke that was made very popular among the development community in town and in the political circles developers cultivated to gain the approvals they needed to turn our town into a city. I know this because it was actually a provincial cabinet minister who first told me the joke. It goes like this:

"What is the difference between an environmentalist and a developer?"

Upon hearing this, one is expected to shrug or say, "Okay, what?"

The answer was: "The environmentalist already has his cabin in the woods."

It was an old saw, one that locals had heard far too many times. But no one where we lived could make the joke work. It just wasn't funny. But when the cabinet minister told it, everyone howled. We also noticed that when local developers told it – to one another at least, which they did time and again in the presence of opponents to their plans – they all roared with laughter.

.

To use a joke to dismiss opponents is standard public relations. But this one, simple as it was, was very effective. It is not really a joke at all and that is why it needs dutiful straight men to laugh to make it work. The joke implies that there are only two groups of people in the world who matter: environmentalists and developers. If you are not an environmentalist, you must be a developer. It is the old "either you are with us or you are against us" trick and it worked very well where we lived. It worked far better than the "NIMBY – not-in-my-back-yard" trick, which no one seemed to buy.

The "cabin in the woods" joke is self-contained in a way that makes it difficult to assail without careful and distanced consideration. It sets up false logic, confirms that false logic and then laughs at anyone who doesn't follow that logic, and it does all of this within seconds. It is meant to insult those who do not support the development prerogative so that they might become emotional at the expense of logic. It works because it demeans those who do not have a cabin in the woods and confounds those who increasingly find themselves, as I did, in a community in which the "woods" described in the joke were either gone or suddenly out of bounds because they had lost their status as public spaces.

But the joke masks an even more profound contradiction, which resides in the fact that a 6,000-square-foot luxury home is hardly a cabin, and that "cabins" of this size displace the "woods" into which they are set. Where I live, there are no more real cabins being built, and the woods are disappearing fast. Isolated clusters of trees not replaced by "cabins" and condos don't last long. They fall naturally, but they are also blowing down now as a result of more frequent and intense windstorms. Or they are being lost to insect infestations stimulated by climate change loosed upon the valley partly as a consequence of the same accelerated human physical and economic mobility that is overwhelming our community culturally. But falling trees and falling for all the traps set for us by developers were not what ultimately cost us our community and our way of life.

Our fifth and greatest failing was far more damaging to us than all the others combined. It was the one that cost us our capacity to build on established local values in the face of wholesale change. Our greatest failing was not that we fell for the developers' spin but that we could not articulate what we meant by local values until after what threatened these values actually materialized and overwhelmed them. While we trumpeted our collective desire to preserve the character of our community, we were not effective in providing local politicians with the language they needed to effect leadership in establishing the town's future. Even though many of these politicians were troubled by the threat of loss as much as any local, they could not find the right words to describe what was happening to us and consequently were as helpless to act in defence of important local values as the rest of us.

Because we could not and did not come to common agreement about what was important about where and how we lived, we were ultimately unable to articulate local interpretations of worthwhile values in a way that could be acted upon in the community planning process. We had no rallying point, no centre, no meeting place, no way of collectively finding our way through to positive common action. Outside interests, of course, capitalized on this. They knew exactly what they wanted; they had a clear, step-by-step strategy for achieving it; and they encouraged inexperienced local developers to adopt these same strategies.

Through outside political influence, the calculated and persistent use of established public relations techniques and the conspicuous display of the kinds of envy-stimulating wealth that could only be created in the short term through speculative real estate price manipulation, developers were able to systematically transform the image of a passionate, educated local community that equated place with cultural identity into its opposite. Where once the town I live in was recognized as a vital community with deep cultural roots well watered by a century of coal mining tradition, this image was quickly transformed through corporate public relations into something radically different. If there was any local resistance at all to the hypermodern vision developers had established for the town and its expanded surroundings, it would come only from a tiny, backward, dwindling and inconsequential constituency of muleheaded hicks who had not yet realized they were fighting impotently against what was undeniably the greatest good for the greatest number of consumers and their friends.

While opponents of what has happened and continues to happen to turn our town into a city may have trouble defending themselves against the charge of being mule-headed, none of us are hicks. The public relations suggestion now is that if you can still afford to live here, lifestyle circumstances will eventually be better than they were before. Few of those who have lived here long are buying that. Neither are all the outsiders who bought into the dream of a cabin in the mountains.

When words fail: the consequences

While the economic influences of growth on municipal governments are well known, the potential impact of rapid growth on local identity is less well understood. In responding to an opportunity to grow, communities often lose things they didn't know were valuable. These impacts are often subtle, at least at first, but they can be important.

The first thing rapid growth generates is a great deal more vehicle traffic. Where I live there are now times of the day when it is actually difficult to get around. There were no traffic lights in this town when I moved here, nor were there any for a decade after we arrived. Now, you can't move without encountering them. If you came from the city, you wouldn't notice. But I do. I don't want to live in a city. I don't want this, and every time I am forced to stop at a red light I am reminded of what I didn't want. But it is not just the traffic lights that bother me. It is the regulated pace of life they bring about. In the context of the city that our town has become, my expectations are now seen as absurd. Not long ago we used to be able to stop even in the middle of Main Street to greet one another. Do that now and someone will lay on the horn until you move.

There is also the matter of public spaces. What was once essentially a commons is now private land. Every last centimetre of highway frontage has been developed. There are designated places where you are allowed to let your dog wander off-leash. There are laws against letting your cat run free. Children can no longer wander at will. The plan is to double again the size of our town in barely 20 years. What freedoms will remain when every lot is developed? How free will locals feel when all the common spaces are gone?

Locals are not just constrained physically as a result of such changes. Place interpenetrates both body and mind. When our spatial realities constrict, our psychological realities are altered as well. There was a time in this town when most locals knew one another. People stopped and talked everywhere they met. It was possible to go to the grocery store or the post office and know everyone. Everyone in the community had the same postal code. All our phone numbers started with the same three digits. A new face was a subject of interest rather than disdain. That is hardly the case today. While it was liberating at first to see so many new faces and to share interests with so many new people, the novelty has not been worth the cost. I do not want to live in the namelessness and facelessness of a city. In this – judging by how many locals are leaving to seek elsewhere the small-town values we lost here – I am not alone.

It is the little things that can affect our identity most – the private relationship we have to place; the space we are able to find for ourselves on the river. It is simple, subtle courtesies that define the comfort with which we fit into our communities; how well we are known; the respect we are accorded by others; the degree to which we sense we belong. The longer we live in a place, the more important these elements become to our identity. In the town I live in we learned that rapid growth can erode these elements of self as defined by place within a surprisingly short time.

As a community, we simply moved too fast and grew too quickly. Interesting and generous people came here with fresh new ideas that could have enriched our way of life in unimaginable ways. But there were too many of them, they arrived too quickly, and too many were just weekenders or occasional visitors. It all happened too fast for the environmental and cultural impacts to be absorbed and for the sense of place to gradually permeate the sensibilities of newcomers in ways that could have allowed them to see the qualities in the mountain West that money cannot buy. Instead, money became the only thing people talked about.

Local social discourse, which was historically dominated by themes such as where one had walked and what landscape and wildlife one had seen, became overwhelmed by crass assessments of how much one's real estate had appreciated in the last month and when it would be appropriate to take the money and run. It was as if the town had suddenly been infected by a deadly case of internal and external parasites. It was as if one of Harry Potter's Dementors had placed their cold, distant and indifferent lips over the warm breath of the town and sucked the very soul out of its sense of community and place. Like a cancer victim fighting for her life, the town's sense of itself shrank inward to a tiny spark of embattled hope. This, we discovered later, was not something unique. The Colorado experience has been validated here where we live. We are seeing that when a mountain town approaches 40 per cent part-time residency, the sense of community begins to implode.

This accelerating implosion has become a serious and very personal problem for those who were born in the town I live in or who moved here for non-urban qualities of place. If to escape the very subdivisions we are now building in our town was the reason you came here in the first place, then how could you relate to what has happened to the place you once loved? How can I, as a lifetime local in this river valley, relate to those who have overwhelmed or skimmed the cream off the top of so much of what is meaningful about where and how I live? How do I recover from the loss I feel?

The town I live in is, quite understandably, not the place I moved to 30 years ago. I never expected it to be. Unfortunately, however, I never anticipated just how much a place can change and how much of what is meaningful about a life and a place can be lost in such a short time. Those of us who have spent the bulk of our lives here have lost the commons that was the surrounding valley. Home place has, not so gradually, contracted from the town and its surroundings to just the town and then to just the subdivision I live in and then to the confines of just our house. As place continues to be overwhelmed and prices continue to rise I fear I will no longer be able to afford our house. I fear displacement, dispossession of all that has defined who I am. Every day, outsiders in rented cars drive up and down our street anxious to buy our home. They want what we have – and then they want us to leave. But there is no place I want to go. How, I ask myself each day, can my identity as a local be sustained in such a place?

The "amenity migration" spin

Terms like "amenity migration" do not describe what happened in my town. In my estimation it is an outrage to characterize what is happening to the West in such egregiously simplistic terms. We did not experience "amenity migration" in the mountain town I live in. What we experienced was outright dispossession. Locals, like the First Nations before us, have been made refugees in their own land. We are hardly alone in this. What is happening here is an infection that is sickening the entire mountain West.

What we could very well be witnessing is the end of the mountain West as we know it. What is happening is nothing less than a complete transformation of landscape and culture.

Terms like "amenity migration" dignify a process that essentially is catastrophic. Despite the apparent best intentions of academics, it is a case, once again, of the language of public relations robbing landscapes and cultures of the capacity and the right to speak for themselves. No amount of public relations spin can make the notion of "amenity migration" stick. The academics who frame dispossession in this way have never felt the heartbeat of a small town. No matter how you promote it, no matter how much spin the developers put on it, a city of wealthy weekenders will never feel or function like a mountain town.

Communities should not count on intellectuals to save them. If we want to save the West, locals will have to do it themselves. Fortunately, we have done it before, which suggests we can do it again. But it won't be easy. Or quick.

Rapid growth in our community was not well planned. What made it difficult to manage was that it wasn't driven from within, but from without. All of the things that happened where I live, however, can happen – will happen – in other communities if residents there are not careful to plan for other possible futures. Whether we like it not, things change. They have to. Growing world populations, increased urban crowding, a global explosion in personal wealth and mobility, and the emergence of investment preferences that double as status symbols make mountain places very attractive. Though it is often masked as tourism development, communities throughout the West are being targeted, whether they like it or not, for their real estate development potential. If you live in one of these communities, the opportunities and the impacts associated with real estate speculation and resort development are coming very soon to a theatre very near you. If this isn't the future you desire for your community, then what might you do?

Saving the West we have

If we want to save what we have, we have to know what we had. To get a sense of what the West was like before we arrived, all we have to do is enter any of our mountain national or provincial parks and compare what we see there with what our communities offer today. While we would never survive today in the isolation of the mountain wilderness as various First Peoples did before us, we can see from the landscape that exists in our protected places what has been passed down to us from previous generations. There is much we can put into relief by comparing what we had to what we expect today.

The extraordinary example of the Canadian Rocky Mountain Parks World Heritage Site suggests that even rapid change need not threaten our way of life. It is possible to balance development and use with ecosystem protection. We can save where we live – but only if we love it and are not afraid to act on that love. The American writer Terry Tempest Williams reminds us that "it is a vulnerable enterprise to feel deeply," and that we may not survive our affections. Williams feels we are being taught to hoard our spirit so that when a landscape we care about is lost, our hearts are not broken because we never risked giving our love away.

The onslaught of public relations and aggressive self-interest in our society has made us fear and suspect our deepest feelings of connection within us. By bottling up our cravings and our love and confining them within, as Williams says in *An Unspoken Hunger*, we keep ourselves "'docile and loyal and obedient'" and we settle for or accept the inevitability of loss of what is at the root of our connection with place. Long-suffering locals perpetuate this docility and obedience when we employ length of residence as a means of robbing passionate newcomers of the ability to feel as strongly as we do about the landscapes we share. This does not mean, however, that length of residence and deep connections to place aren't important. They are a foundation of localness we need to encourage in the mountain West.

In Canada, we have a habit of leaving places when they no longer suit us. We realize our world has changed when we can no longer relate to ourselves by way of where we live. Instead of staying and defending what is important about where and how we want to live, we pack up and leave. The town up the valley was good once. When it changed, people who cared about place and community moved to where I live. Now that the town I live in has changed, people who seek place are looking at Golden in British Columbia. People in Golden are looking at Fernie and Nelson. The people in Nelson are looking to the Slocan. The people in the Slocan Valley have no place else to go.

We seem to be always searching for what we can't have or keep. Wherever we go, we bring the problems we were trying to escape. We are running out of places to run to. It is time, perhaps, to make a stand. It is time to define what is important about where and how we live, and to stand by those values in defining our future. It is time to define our heritage and make the link between it and what we want the future to be.

In the decade before "the boom," there was so much talk in our community about doing everything possible to ensure we didn't become another tourist town. We failed to realize that we could become another city instead. Whatever mountain character our community may have had, it has lost, at least for now. It is not the West I want and hoped for. It is not the West I want to leave to my children.

The pervasive presence of outside developers and speculators suggests it may well be that a different kind of protest is needed to mourn the loss of local place in the mountain West and to defend against future losses. That protest might well begin through the rejection of public planning processes imposed from outside. Those living in a mountain town that is under threat of being overwhelmed may want to take the time, before the home invasion begins, to consider what is important to them about where and how they live and see whether or not they might be able to make that the attraction. Do not expect standard municipal planning processes to accommodate this. Current laws, from World Trade Organization and North American Free Trade Agreement rules right down to municipal government ordinances, may presently make it illegal to actively defend where you live. In order to be successful in creating the West we want, communities will have to reform these processes.

We have to re-establish community and inter-jurisdictional dialogue as a means of affirming a new vision of the mountain West rather than as a tool for simply endorsing the self-interest that is currently eroding the common good.

Mounting a different kind of protest

Communities that want to save themselves may need to get thoughtful and influential locals together to articulate a common appreciation of place so that political leaders clearly know and can fully express what values and traditions they should aim to preserve through your community's already existing development and land-use planning processes before the threat is upon them. In order to slow development to a pace at which it can be accepted and embraced by locals, I propose that a community ask itself three questions. All three relate to whether or not you have ascribed appropriate value to what you already have in terms of built heritage, local values and traditions and sense of place.

The first question is: Will locals be able to afford to live in your community after full buildout, and will they want to stay?

The second question a town facing huge outside development activity should ask is: Where will the dispossessed go?

The third question a community under siege may wish to pose is this: What do you want your community to be like after it grows?

After agreeing on what is important about where and how you live, define the kinds of economic development you want to have, and determine the compromises and sacrifices you are prepared to make to ensure the kind of economic development you want is possible. Then go after the kinds of visitors and newcomers who will be willing to share your generosity in ways that need not destroy local cultural traditions and sense of place. Small mountain towns have a great deal to offer, and standing up for place will make where you live even more desirable.

Canadian poet Don McKay posits that place is where memory begins, and memory is how we place ourselves in the time in which we live. He describes home place as a practice or set of practices related to the developing connection between self and the world. It is in our home place that we build paths through time and space. According to McKay, place becomes place by acquiring real or imagined borders. Change occurs to the extent that the membrane between place and what lies outside is permeated. But what happens when that membrane isn't just permeated, but violated?

In *Deactivated West 100*, McKay argues that perhaps it is time to apply the "catch and release" principle to place. Perhaps we should discourage people who visit the last, best small communities from pulling place out of its native waters and gutting it by buying it up and developing it for their occasional weekend consumption. Perhaps we should make it fashionable for those who have trouble finding new places to park their money and prestige to just dip their net into the waters of place and then return their endangered catch to the stream. If not, then perhaps we should be encouraging them to actually stay if they love the place so much. We should appeal to their higher ideals and ask the world's wealthy to contribute to place rather than replacing it.

We have to expect our communities to change. In fact, we need them to change. But growth shouldn't have to mean diminishment and loss of the central founding values of place. Growth at the expense of the sense of community and relationship to place is growth in name only. A community is worth living in only to the extent that its residents know and care about where they live and are prepared to make a stand for the quality of life that means the most to them.

Leaders like Mayor Randall McNair in Fernie, British Columbia, are right to encourage people who start as weekenders to become full-time locals. As has been witnessed in the town I live in, visitors and weekenders can contribute significantly to a community if their numbers don't overwhelm and if enough of them stay with the proper aim of building on the good that is already present rather than simply replacing it with what they sought to escape where they used to live. From the moment their numbers overwhelm and they take over culturally, however, it isn't long until the qualities of place that attracted them are diminished or disappear. It is not impossible to restore these qualities in a community, but it is very difficult.

Recovering and rebuilding

In looking at what we lost in the town where I live, it is possible to identify obvious qualities that might be worth fighting for if you are forced to stand up for the mountain place you live in.

It is worthwhile to fight to protect spectacular, unimpaired and unobstructed land- and water-scapes. Visitors aren't going to cross a continent or an ocean to see landscapes and communities that are as compromised as the ones they have at home. Know when you have something amazing.

Take pride in the unique character of local architecture and established patterns of land use. This unique aspect of place is expressed in part by the obvious absence of the universal tourism architecture typified by chain hotels and restaurant franchises. It is expressed also in the way standard urban real estate grid patterns have not been allowed to interrupt the sensuous, organic relationship between buildings and their surroundings.

I wish, for example, that where I live was laid out like the old part of Rossland, British Columbia, instead of being just like any subdivision you would find in Toronto or Calgary.

Fight to the death to prevent tacky highway strips. As built environments lacking human qualities encroach upon the authentic ones given to us by nature or by our cultural heritage, people are having more and more difficulty establishing and maintaining a unique personal identity and sense of place. Realize that local identity and culture matter.

And whatever you do, don't lose your sense of humour. Laughter can be an expression of the utmost joy. Local mountain humour is earthy, spontaneous and uncontainable in its big-heartedness. I was once down in Waterton just after a 120 km/h wind had blown for three days. One woman told me she had become so used to it that the only reason she noticed it was so windy was that a pair of ducks flew over her like jet planes. No sooner had she said that than an old cowboy leaned over and declared dryly, "What you saw was them eider jets."

Keeping our language is far more important than we may know. We have our own language in many parts of the mountain West. Words like glacier, tarn, moraine, col, pass and fault are words unique to mountain place. So are words like grizzly, cougar, wolf and wolverine. Our identity as a people is also defined by words like trail, switchback and summit cairn.

To preserve what is essential about where and how we live, we must preserve this language. The loss of words can lead to the loss of the things those words stand for. The devaluation of words makes for the devaluation of the things words describe. A vicious circle is created from which there is no escape.

With fewer words to describe the places that surround us, it becomes harder to justify saving them. As these places vanish from our direct experience, the need for a language to describe them vanishes as well. In his book *The Nature of Generosity*, William Kittredge warns that languages can decay and die. Once the language people employed to tell the story of who they are vanishes, sense of self can be lost. People can become less than they once were.

We are what we say and what we sing. But we are no longer unique if what we say and sing is the same as what everyone else says or sings. If all you think about, all you talk about, is investment, occupancy, return on equity, how long will it be before what you say and sing is what everyone else is saying and singing?

Preserve local names and stories. As Kittredge has also pointed out, "Naming helps people witness themselves and reflect on what they've seen. It is the beginning of talking to ourselves, that most primal business, in which we invent and reinvent ourselves all day long, incessantly thinking and feeling, talking ourselves into being. Saying local names and reinventing our stories is an endless, non-stop search for ourselves."

Places also come to exist in our imaginations because of stories. Having a "sense of self" means possessing a set of stories about who we are and where and how we live. The mountain West is a place of myth, legend and story. Kittredge tells us that "the stories we tell are important because they remind us all to love ourselves, one another and the world."

I also believe it is important to keep things local and to preserve local service traditions. In my opinion it is better to encourage small, locally owned businesses rather than big operations owned by outside interests that have targeted where you live as a profitable outpost of globalization. Important decisions affecting our future are made in office towers in Toronto and Calgary. These decisions seldom respect our uniqueness. But by offering the same products and services everyone else does, we have become placeless.

Standardization of hospitality styles can also be part of placelessness. Everywhere in Canada, tourism people treat you pretty much the same because they have all taken the same hospitality training. I like to visit rural mountain communities because I don't have to put up with homogenized standards of service and hospitality. Though it is not always sophisticated, what you get here are the good manners and genuine respect you would expect when visiting friends.

If these are the kinds of qualities mountain communities want to retain, then why are we so rapidly losing the unique character that symbolizes the West in the world's imagination? If governance that preserves strong local identity based on respect for place makes such long-term good sense, why is it so hard to do? It is perhaps because we have not valued identity and sense of place to the extent that we might.

It is not too late to do so, however. It is not too late to build further on what is important about where and how we live and to sustain those qualities as both way of life and attraction. I believe it is still entirely possible to create a culture commensurate with the grandeur of the landscapes we live in. All we have to do is want to.

Where I live it will take time and vision to make a true home and a real community out of what has essentially been for decades an enormous construction site. A community, as everyone knows, is more than just built forms. In many ways, it is far easier to build houses and streets than it is to build the kind of local associations and cultural traditions that make it worthwhile living in those houses and pleasurable to walk those streets. It will never be what it was before, but it can still be a worthwhile place to live, even for long-time locals.

With prosperity temporarily upon us, it is a good time to reconsider what kind of West we want: not just the economic, cultural or virtual landscape we want to create, but the physical West that will provide our inspiration and our solace and shape our deepest identity. It is not just about money. In making our stand for where and how we live, we must reach into our hearts for the deepest expression of our passion for place. We have to find words for our epiphany, and then find the courage to stand by them. There is no better place to do that than in the largest accessible, ecologically intact mountain region in the world.

Becoming native to place

In his book *Becoming Native to this Place*, Wes Jackson argues that, in North America at least, it has never been a goal to become native to where you live and to establish deep ties to all aspects of place. He claims that only now, almost too late, are we beginning to perceive the necessity of establishing such relationships.

In order to preserve even the possibility of an enduring sense of place, Jackson contends that we have to slow down our aimless, wandering pursuit of upward mobility at any cost and find a home, dig in and aim for some kind of enduring relationship with the ecological realities of the surrounding landscape. Jackson believes we have to somehow reverse the Western frontier tradition of picking up and leaving the moment a place is no longer what we want it to be. We have to learn to stop running away. We have to stay and to stand up for where we live.

Jackson believes the only way we can restore anything that will remotely resemble our former world is to become native again in our relationship to where we live. We have to become grounded in where we live, establish our own identities through sense of place and stand up for local values. We have to have confidence in what we are and what we can become. In this period of great change we have to trust in the resilience of Western landscapes and Western people.

The frontier era is over and the West awaits its next historical age. We have to create the next best West. We forget sometimes that with each decision we make and with our every action, we are making history. With each decision we make concerning the future, we are remaking our West. We should not be satisfied to simply accept what we get. We should build on our already considerable achievement by realizing the value of what we already have and have done. We should use our great success in protecting mountain places and local cultural traditions that matter to us as a crystal around which we create the West we want next. We have done it once. There is no reason we can't do it again.

What was worthwhile to the founding generations of locals in the mountain West may not exist much longer unless we take care in teaching newcomers and subsequent generations the historical lessons that took us centuries to learn. Principal among those lessons is that in this landscape our identity can never be completely defined by development. What we save ultimately matters as much as anything we might build. We are not made entirely whole by what we earn or by the comforts and privileges what we earn may afford us. True and enduring wealth still ultimately resides, in the mountain West at least, in making peace with place, for only in so doing can we make peace with ourselves.

Bookshelf

Bass, Rick. *The Book of Yaak*. Boston: Houghton Mifflin Co., 1996.

Crichton, Michael. *Travels*. New York: Knopf, 1988.

Jackson, Wes. *Becoming Native to this Place*. Lexington: University Press of Kentucky, 1994.

Kittredge, William. *The Nature of Generosity*. New York: Knopf, 2000.

Lawrence, T.E. *Seven Pillars of Wisdom*. London: Penguin, 2000.

McKay, Don. *Deactivated West 100*. Kentville, NS: Gaspereau Press, 2005.

Rees, Ronald. *New and Naked Land: Making the Prairies Home*. Saskatoon, Sask.: Western Producer Prairie Books, 1988.

Stegner, Wallace. *The American West as Living Space*. Ann Arbor: University of Michigan Press, 1987.

———. *Angle of Repose*. New York: Penguin, 1992.

———. *The Bluebird Sings at Lemonade Springs*. New York: Modern Library, 2002.

———. *The Sound of Mountain Water*. New York: Penguin, 1997.

———. *Wolf Willow*. New York: Penguin, 2000.

Williams, Terry Tempest. *An Unspoken Hunger: Stories from the Field*. New York: Pantheon Books, 1994.

Worster, Donald. *Nature's Economy: A History of Ecological Ideas*. 2nd ed. Cambridge and New York: Cambridge University Press, 1994.